WITHDRAWN

LIBRARIES

D1468123

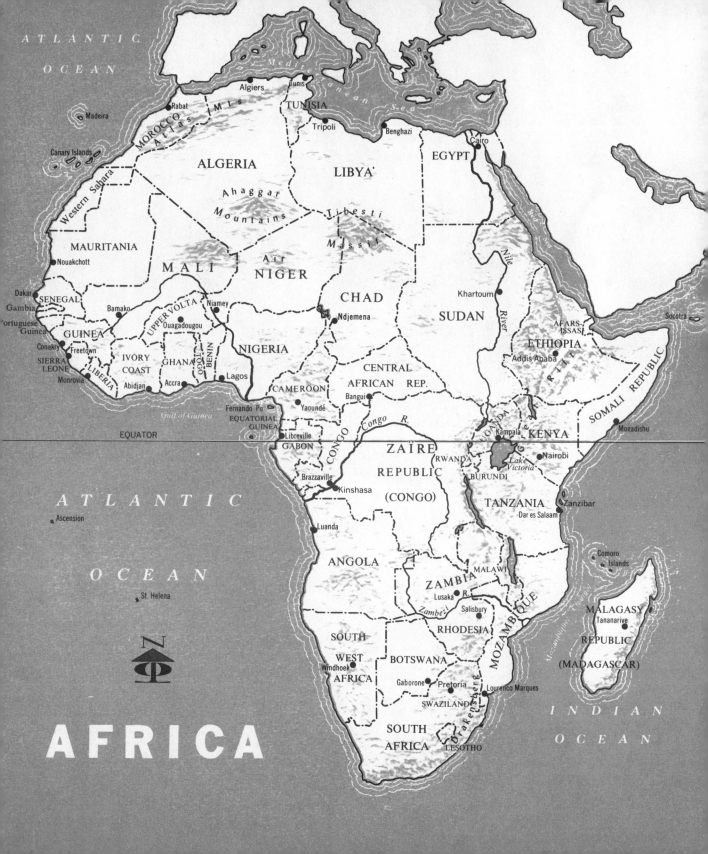

MAURITANIA

by ALLAN CARPENTER
and JAMES HUGHES

Consulting Editor
John Rowe
Department of History
Northwestern University
Evanston, Illinois

 CHILDRENS PRESS, CHICAGO

THE ENCHANTMENT OF AFRICA

Available now: Benin (Dahomey), Botswana, Burundi, Cameroon, Central African Republic, Chad, Congo (Brazzaville), Egypt, Equatorial Guinea, Gambia, Gabon, Ghana, Guinea, Ivory Coast, Kenya, Lesotho, Liberia, Libya, Malagasy Republic (Madagascar), Malawi, Mali, Mauritania, Morocco, Niger, Rhodesia, Rwanda, Senegal, Sierra Leone, Sudan, Swaziland, Tanzania, Togo, Tunisia, Uganda, Upper Volta, Zaire Republic (Congo Kinshasa), Zambia
Planned for the future: Equatorial Guinea, Ethiopia, Nigeria, Somali Republic, South Africa

BOARD OF ADVISERS, THE PROGRAM OF AFRICAN STUDIES
NORTHWESTERN UNIVERSITY, EVANSTON, ILLINOIS

Abraham Demoz, Ph.D., Director
Frances A. Leary, Ph. D., Assistant Director
Beth V. Miller, Staff

Ibrahim Abu-Lughod, Ph.D.
Janet Abu-Lughod, Ph.D.
Ethel Albert, Ph.D.
Andrew J. Beattie, Ph.D.
John H. Beckstrom, L.L.M.
Jack Berry, Ph.D.
P.J. Bohannan, D. Phil.
Daniel Britz, M.A.
Dennis Brutus, B.A.
Donald T. Campbell, Ph.D.
Jan Carew, Professor
Remi Clignet, Doctorat de Recherches
Ronald Cohen, Ph.D.
David C. Culver, Ph.D.
George Dalton, Ph.D.
Ralph E. Dolkart, M.D.
Fredric L. DuBow, Ph.D.
Edward B. Espenshade, Ph.D.
Morris Goodman, Ph.D.
Ted R. Gurr, Ph.D.
Errol Harris, D. Litt.
Peter J. Jacobi, M.S.J.
Raymond A. Kliphardt, M.S.

Asmarom Legesse, Ph.D.
Sidney J. Levy, Ph.D.
Judith McAfee, M.L.S.
David Michener, M.S.
Johannes Mlela, M.P.A.
Leon Moses, Ph.D.
Rae Moore Moses, Ph.D.
John F. Ohl, Ph.D.
John N. Paden, Ph.D.
Hans E. Panofsky, M.S.
Arrand Parsons, Ph.D.
Edithe Potter, Ph.D.
John Rowe, Ph.D.
Albert H. Rubenstein, Ph.D.
Robert I. Schneideman, Ph.D.
Walter Scott, Ph.D.
Frank Spalding, J.D.
Richard Spears, Ph.D.
Lindley J. Stiles, Ed.D.
Stuart Struever, Ph.D.
Sterling Stuckey, Ph.D.
Ibrahim Sundiata, Ph.D.
Taddesse Tamrat, Ph.D.
Ralph L. Westfall, Ph.D.
E.H.T. Whitten, Ph.D.
Robert Wilkinson, Ph.D.
Ivor Wilks, Ph.D.
Frank Willett, M.A.

ACKNOWLEDGMENTS

Secretariat General—Artisanat-Tourism; Mme. Jean Cheikh Abdallahi, Chief of Service for Tourism, Nouakchott; Embassy of the United States of America, Nouakchott; Mission of the Islamic Republic of Mauritania to the United Nations, New York; Embassy of the Islamic Republic of Mauritania, Washington, D.C.

Cover Photograph: Mauritanian young men, Allan Carpenter
Frontispiece: Men in the market, *La Mauritania En Marche*

Project Editor: Joan Downing
Assistant Editor: Mary Reidy
Manuscript Editor: Janis Fortman
Map Artist: Eugene Dardeyn

Copyright © 1977. Regensteiner Publishing Enterprises, Inc.
All rights reserved. Printed in the U.S.A.
Published simultaneously in Canada.

1 2 3 4 5 6 7 8 9 10 11 12 R 85 84 83 82 81 80 79 78 77

LIBRARY OF CONGRESS
CATALOGING IN PUBLICATION DATA

Carpenter, John Allan, 1917-
    Mauritania.
    (Enchantment of Africa)

    SUMMARY: An introduction to the geography, history, government, economy, culture, and people of the African country that is three-fourths desert.
    1. Mauritania—Juvenile literature. [1. Mauritania]
I. Hughes, James, 1934-   joint author.
II. Title.
DT553.M2C37   966' .1   76-53010
ISBN 0-516-04576-8

LIBRARY
The University of Texas
At San Antonio

Contents

A True Story to Set the Scene

THE DAY THE SUN BURNED OUT

For several weeks, Ahmed and his family had been traveling slowly across the central desert lands of Mauritania. The trip was an annual event; this was the time of the year when the family would sell their surplus goats and camels to the merchants at Atar. Many other nomadic families were also on their way to Atar—a busy, old trading center in the northwest. Ahmed's family had joined a few families and formed a caravan. Every day more families had joined them, and the caravan was now quite large.

Although Ahmed was eleven years old, he had vivid memories of his previous trips to Atar. He was fascinated by the many people who gathered at the market. The people all wore different clothes, spoke different languages, and had different customs. As usual, Ahmed was very excited about the animal trades.

In only a few days, Ahmed and his family would reach Atar. This morning Ahmed's older brother had said that something very unusual was going to happen to the sun that day. In a teasing manner, his brother had told Ahmed, "Today at noon the sun will burn out! No longer will there be a sun to warm the desert and

The north and northeast of Mauritania is desert, with huge stretches of sand dunes. There are few landmarks in the desert to guide travelers. The landscape is always changing because of ergs. Ergs are piles of sand that actually change their entire shape and location as a result of the powerful desert winds that blow them about.

MICHAEL ROBERTS

It is difficult to navigate when the desert sands are blowing.

bring light to the land." Although Ahmed sensed that his brother was joking, he was still curious and a bit frightened about what was supposed to happen to the sun that day!

Around eleven o'clock that morning, the caravan spotted an encampment on a hill not far from the oasis of Atar. A group of Africans and Europeans were busily setting up strange-looking pieces of equipment on one of the high sand dunes nearby. The strangers' Mauritanian guide came forward and greeted Ahmed's father in the customary Islamic tradition. Then he introduced Ahmed's father to the African and European scientists.

Ahmed's father signaled the caravan to rest. The older men of the caravan decided that the group would remain near the strangers' camp until late afternoon, and then they would accompany the strangers on their trip back to Atar.

As the older men in the caravan rested their weary camels, some of the children gathered around the busy strangers. Ahmed was particularly curious about a large, tubular instrument that a European man was looking through. Noticing Ahmed's curiosity, the man motioned Ahmed to come forward. But Ahmed was too shy. Ahmed's older brother told the man how Ahmed had been teased about what was expected to happen to the sun at noon that day. With his brother's prodding, Ahmed finally approached the man with the strange-looking instrument.

Though the European scientist could speak only a little Arabic, he tried to explain to Ahmed the scientific reasons for the forthcoming event. He explained that

Ahmed is always fascinated by the people who gather at the market.

Surplus goats are sold at the market.

MICHAEL ROBERTS

the sun and moon travel in circular orbits around the earth; at noon the moon would pass between the sun and the earth, blocking the sun's light. He told Ahmed that the darkness would last only a short time.

The scientist then positioned the huge telescope so Ahmed could look through it. He put a special colored lens on one end, shading the brightness of the sun. Soon Ahmed was able to see the sun and the moon through the telescope. As he kept watching, the sun and moon appeared to move closer and closer to each other. Then the scientist looked through the telescope again. Ahmed could see that all the scientists were very busy. The scientist had told Ahmed that motion-picture cameras would record the strange event in the sky.

As Ahmed watched the busy men, gradually the sky became darker. The scientist let Ahmed gaze through the telescope again. Sure enough—the moon was passing in front of the sun, blocking its rays. For seven minutes, it almost seemed

like night on the desert. Even the camels grew restless and made awkward cries, as if sensing the unusual occurrence. But Ahmed was no longer frightened. He had seen the eclipse. Ahmed was proud to have looked through the telescope and understood what had happened. It was neither a trick nor a disaster, as his brother had teased him that morning. It was a scientific event that had taken place in the sky. At supper that night, Ahmed explained to his family what an eclipse really was, as he described vividly the sights he had seen through the powerful telescope.

On that day—June 30, 1973—many other scientists all across Africa carefully observed this total eclipse of the sun as its path crossed from Mauritania into Mali, southern Algeria, Niger, Chad, and Kenya. All the people in those areas saw the eclipse, too. Though many of them did not understand it. Some of the people thought that a spirit was angry with them, and they were afraid. But not Ahmed!

INTERNATIONAL BANK FOR RECONSTRUCTION AND DEVELOPMENT

While many changes are taking place in Mauritania, some traditions remain. A Moorish woman, in traditional dress, watches a bulldozer at work.

11

LA REPUBLIQUE ISLAMIQUE DE MAURITANIA

In the central desert belt are vast, barren sandy plains with occasional small scrub trees.

12

The Face of the Land

THE MYSTERIOUS SANDS
OF THE DESERT

Since people were first able to travel into the interior of the Sahara, this land has been described as "mysterious." One reason for the desert's mystery might be its ever-changing landscape, which is caused by *ergs,* or shifting sand dunes. Ergs are huge piles of sand that actually change

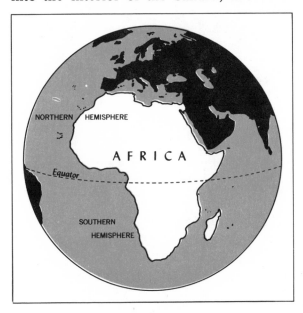

their entire shape and location as a result of the powerful desert winds that blow them about. Because of the shifting ergs, the desert never looks the same. Desert travelers cannot trust their memories of the landscape as a sure means of retracing their paths through the desert. It is easy to get lost in this vast desert, for there are few landmarks to guide a traveler along. Thus, the shifting sands help give the Sahara its reputation of mystery.

But not all of Mauritania is desert land. In the south, the Senegal River forms a lush, green subtropical valley. But this quickly thins out to desert, and the barren Sahara covers all of central and northern Mauritania—three-fourths of the country. Located in northwestern Africa, the Islamic Republic of Mauritania occupies approximately 419,231 square miles of land—about the size of Arizona, New Mexico, Colorado, and Utah combined.

Bordered on the west by the Atlantic Ocean, Mauritania has about four hundred miles of coastline. To the northwest is the Western Sahara and to the northeast is Algeria. The Republic of Mali borders Mauritania on the east and southeast, and the Senegal River forms the southern border, dividing Mauritania from Senegal.

THE GREEN BELT

In the south, the Senegal River valley forms a long, narrow belt of land that is basically subtropical. The region receives almost twenty-five inches of rain annually, and its soil is suitable for agriculture. The land near the river valley supports a lush forest, but farther north, the vegetation gradually becomes more sparse. There are fewer trees and great stretches of grasslands where herds of animals graze. For hundreds of years, a settled,

MAP KEY

Adrar Hills, D-3, D-4
Ain Ben Tili, B-4
Akjoujt, E-2
Aleg, F-2
Atar, E-2
'Ayoûn el 'Atroûs, F-4

Bassi Kounou, G-6
Bir Morgrein, B-3
Bogué, F-2
Boutilimit, F-2

Cape Tafarit, E-1
Cape Timiris, E-1
Chinguetti, E-3

El Mreyyé, D-5

Fort Gouraud, D-3

Iguidi Dunes, B-5

Kaédi, F-2
Kankossa, G-3
Karakoro River, F-3, G-3
Kediet Ijill, D-3
Kiffa, F-3
Kolimbine River, G-3, G-4
Koumbi-Seleh, G-5

Leggah, F-2

Mbout, G-3
Mederdra, F-1
Moudjéria, F-3

Néma, F-5
Nouadhibou, D-1
Nouakchott, F-1
Nouamrhar, E-1

Ouadane, D-3
Oualâta, F-5
Ouarane Dunes, E-3, E-4

Rhallamane Dunes, B-3, B-4, C-3, C-4

Rosso, F-1

Sahara Desert, D-5, D-6
Sélibaby, G-3
Senegal River, F-1, F-2, G-2, G-3

Tamchaket, F-4
Tichit, F-4
Tidjikdja, E-3
Tiguesmat Hills, B-4, B-5, C-4, C-5
Timbédra, G-5

Zouîrât, D-3

14

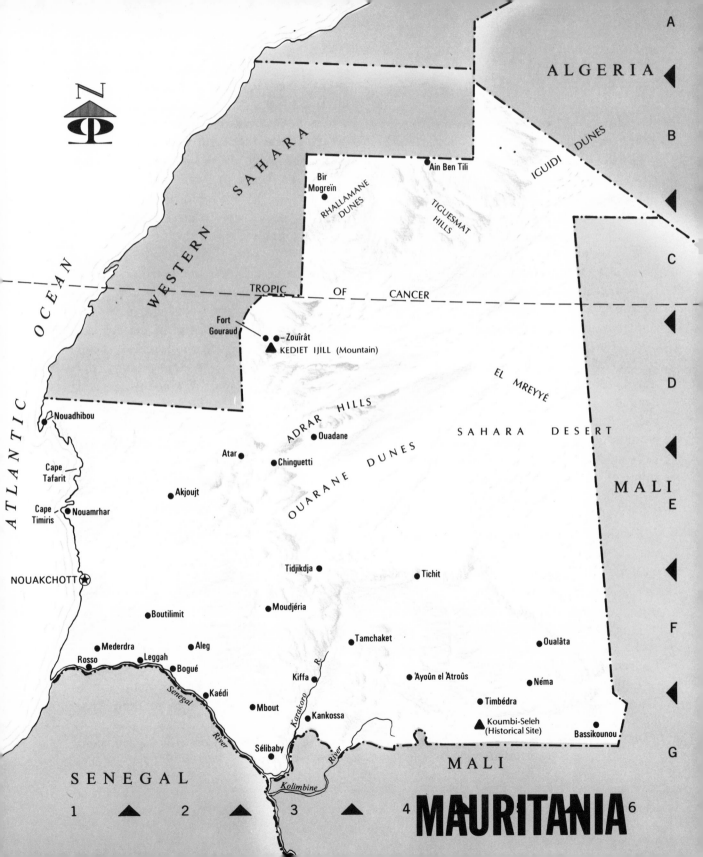

A

ALGERIA

B

WESTERN SAHARA

Ain Ben Tili

Bir Mogreïn

RHALLAMANE DUNES

IGUIDI DUNES

TIGUESMAT HILLS

C

ATLANTIC OCEAN

TROPIC OF CANCER

Fort Gouraud

Zouîrât

KEDIET IJILL (Mountain)

EL MREYYÉ

D

Nouadhibou

ADRAR HILLS

SAHARA DESERT

MALI

Cape Tafarit

Atar

Ouadane

Chinguetti

OUARANE DUNES

E

Akjoujt

Cape Timiris

Nouamrhar

NOUAKCHOTT

Tidjikdja

Tichit

F

Boutilimit

Moudjéria

Mederdra

Aleg

Tamchaket

Oualâta

Rosso

Leggah

Bogué

Kiffa

'Ayoûn el 'Atroûs

Néma

Kaédi

Karakoro R.

Timbédra

Mbout

Kankossa

Koumbi-Seleh (Historical Site)

Bassikounou

G

Sélibaby

Senegal River

Kolimbine

River

MALI

SENEGAL

1   2   3   4   **MAURITANIA** 6

agricultural form of life has existed in the Senegal River valley.

THE VAST DESERT LANDS

North of the savanna lands of the Senegal River valley, the grasslands thin out into desert. Vast, barren sandy plains, with occasional patches of grass or small scrub trees, make up the central desert belt. Farther north and northeast, complete desert conditions prevail. The land becomes extremely arid, and huge stretches of sand dunes appear. Though some dunes are permanent, others are ergs. Parts of the land are extremely rocky, with dangerously thin outcroppings. High, rocky pinnacles add to the dramatic appearance of this land. The rocky plateaus of the Sahara rise to heights of fifteen hundred feet. Mauritania's most famous peak is F'dérik, part of a range of mountains called Kediet Ijill. The range rises three thousand feet above sea level.

Erosion has been a prime factor in carving out some of the spectacular rock formations in this harsh desert land. The strong winds and the extreme temperatures help the erosion process. During the heat of the day, the sun's rays cause some rocks to heat up to almost 200 degrees Fahrenheit. At night, temperatures drop rapidly, often falling as low as 45 degrees. These extremes in temperature cause some rocks to expand and contract, which can result in explosion and disintegration of the rocks.

The Sahara has not always been barren desert: it was lush with vegetation during the Stone Age. With numerous streams and river beds, it was well watered. Animals and people lived in this beautiful land. But as time went on, changes in the world's climate caused the Sahara to dry up.

Sudden cloudbursts are common in the desert. Although the water that accompanies a storm is always welcomed, many desert people are also fearful of the storms. If a storm is too sudden and forceful, it can cause great damage. In desert lands, the ground is usually baked solid by the sun and does not easily absorb water. When a storm occurs in the highlands, excess water races forcefully downhill, often causing floods and even death to people traveling or camping in the normally dry, ancient streambeds.

THE GREAT DROUGHT

In 1969 a terrible drought began throughout all of the Sahara, including Mauritania. Every year for more than five years, the rains either failed completely, occurred at the wrong time of year, or were so minimal that they were of no value to the people. The drought crept silently into the lives of more than fifty

Sandy silver beaches extend for hundreds of miles along the Atlantic Coast. So far no resort facilities have been built, but there are limitless possibilities for tourism.

ALLAN CARPENTER

ALLAN CARPENTER

A drought in the early 1970s forced many desert dwellers to take refuge in the city.

ALLAN CARPENTER

ALLAN CARPENTER

Tent cities, tin and cardboard shacks on the outskirts of Nouakchott, sometimes even on the grounds of the mosques, housed refugees. Little employment or comfort could be found for these people in the capital city, which barely had enough for its normal population.

LA MAURITANIE

Survival in the desert is difficult. Above: Strange rock formations are caused by erosion. Right: During the rainy season, wells are all important for travelers. Below: Not much vegetation survives in the desert.

LA REPUBLIQUE ISLAMIQUE DE MAURITANIA

ALLAN CARPENTER

million Africans. Millions of people starved because of the drought, as well as millions of cattle and sheep. People all over the world sent aid—food and seed —to the drought-stricken victims, but many areas are hard to reach. Even when the drought is ended it takes a long time before food stockpiles can be built up to their previous levels.

CLIMATE AND SEASON

Mauritania's climate is generally hot and dry—except for the Senegal River valley. In the extreme desert regions of the Sahara, there is usually less than two inches of rain a year. Desert temperatures are quite extreme. From November through March, temperatures may rise to 100 degrees during the day and drop to as low as freezing at night. From April through October, the temperatures are much higher, ranging from a high of 120 degrees to a low of 60 degrees in a twenty-four-hour period.

The central desert regions get slightly more rain—from four to twelve inches a year. Temperatures range from a high of 120 degrees to a low of 50 degrees. Severe hot winds blow into this area from the interior of the Sahara. The area of the central desert that borders the Atlantic Ocean is cooled by ocean breezes.

Along the subtropical Senegal River valley the climate is quite different than that of the desert lands to the north. Here rains fall in quantities of twelve to twenty-six inches annually, and there are floods during the heavy rainy season. Humidity is often quite high in this part of the country. Temperatures here are usually in the eighties, and there is less difference between day and night temperatures than in the desert.

Four Children of Mauritania

ZAKIA OF LEGGAH

Zakia is the youngest girl in a farming family that lives in Leggah, one of the many villages scattered along the Senegal River in southern Mauritania. Zakia's family has lived in the same location for as long as any living member of the family can recall.

Eleven-year-old Zakia recently became an aunt when her brother and his young wife had their first son. As is customary among the Sarakole people, the sister of the father chooses a first name for the baby. Zakia was asked to honor her nephew with a name of her choice. She was thrilled with this honor and responsibility.

As soon as the baby was born, Zakia's sister-in-law remained in seclusion at her mother's home. For seven days the two women stayed home, making sure that no harm would come to the helpless baby.

Land along the Senegal River is suitable for farming and grazing.

ALLAN CARPENTER

Zakia's mother bought the ingredients for the couscous *at the market.*

During that time, Zakia and many other members of the family were preparing for the festivities that would accompany the baptism, which would be held on the eighth day. On the seventh day, Zakia's brother announced to the village elders his plans for the child's baptism. The church leader from the local mosque was asked to officiate at the ceremony. Everyone was invited to the mother-in-law's home.

Zakia's mother had agreed to help prepare food for the occasion; much food would be needed for the couple's many friends and relatives. Zakia helped her mother cut up the carrots, onions, tomatoes, peppers, and bits of lamb that would be used for the *couscous* (lamb stew). Many friends contributed fish and chickens, which would also be used for stews.

Zakia had chosen the ancient name "Makha" for her nephew. According to traditional beliefs, a once powerful king of their people was also honored with this name. The holy man from the mosque would select a Muslim saint's name for the child. The new infant would receive a fine welcome into his new life. Zakia was very excited about her new nephew.

Zakia knew she would spend a lot of time with her nephew in the days ahead. Sarakole girls are expected to help the mothers care for the babies. Zakia had often fed and clothed her younger brothers, as well as other relatives' children. When the older women were busy working in the fields, Zakia usually took care of five or six younger children.

Not all of Zakia's time, however, is spent working. She spends her free time with her many girl friends in the village. Sometimes the girls gather together after their afternoon rest. By this time, the sun is losing its powerful heat, and there is often a cool breeze. The girls usually sit underneath a large tree, telling stories or singing songs or making up riddles. Zakia especially enjoys when the girls take turns adding new verses to some of their traditional folk songs. Sometimes they try to see who can create the funniest words.

Most of the girls are required to be home by dusk in order to help cook the evening meal. Zakia usually grinds the millet early in the day, so at dusk all she has to do is carry water to the cooking area and lend a hand when her mother needs assistance.

SIDI OF NOUAKCHOTT

Sidi was not sure if he liked living in Nouakchott, the capital city of Mauritania. But because of his father's new job, he had to live there. His father had recently

Only about 10 percent of the population lives in cities and towns.

ALLAN CARPENTER

MICHAEL ROBERTS

Sidi was amazed at all the construction that was being done in Nouakchott. Here a new home is being built.

been promoted to an important position in the Ministry of Information; he helped prepare the bilingual newsletters distributed daily by this agency.

Sidi and his mother had only recently arrived in the city, and both of them knew very few people. At first, Sidi and his mother had spent countless hours exploring the city's many strange, new sights. Sidi had been amazed at the huge machines and trucks that were used in the construction of new buildings. He had never seen such large buildings and so many people. Sidi found himself feeling

very lonely, even though he was surrounded by crowds of people.

Sidi thought of his home and the people he knew there. It was only two weeks since he and his mother had left the village and come to the city on the bus. The bus had been full of people, suitcases, fruit, and animals. The ride was rough and noisy, as the bus bounced over the dirt road while chickens squawked and babies cried. Sidi had been sad to leave his many friends and his family. He hoped he could see them again sometime soon, but he didn't know when.

26

One Friday Sidi went with his father to the mosque for evening prayers. With his cap on his head, Sidi walked quietly next to his father. Once at the mosque, they removed their sandals and prepared themselves for their prayers. Sidi finished before his father, so he went outside to wait. Sitting on a bench, Sidi watched many other young men entering the mosque.

Soon Sidi's father appeared with the holy man of the mosque, who greeted Sidi. After acknowledging the holy man in the correct Islamic manner, Sidi was told that there was room in the school for one more student. The holy man asked Sidi if he would like to join the Islamic studies classes at the mosque.

Sidi thought for a minute. He had been well trained in the Arabic language at the mosque in his village, and his parents had helped him memorize passages from the Koran (the Islamic holy book). Sidi thought that he would do well at this new school and that it might be fun. Besides, he would meet some boys his age. The holy man was glad when Sidi agreed to come to the classes.

As Sidi walked home with his father, he looked around the city again. It did not seem as strange as when he had first arrived. Perhaps he was beginning to feel more at home.

SAID OF THE SAHARA

Said (Sah-yeed) is a Moor—one of the people from whom Mauritania took its name. He lives a traditional nomadic life.

His family is almost always moving from one place to another. It would not occur to them to live any other way. The goats, cattle, and camels need grass and water; therefore, the family must constantly move about in search of these items.

Naturally, thirteen-year-old Said is a skilled desert traveler. He knows how to follow directions from the positions of the stars. He knows the desert lands very well and would not want to live elsewhere. Said knows when to feed his animals and when to provide them with drinking water. Besides, he is strong.

Said and his many relatives travel in a caravan. Each major family has its own "tent." A tent represents a family unit, which includes the blood relatives, as well as assistants who travel and work for the family. These people are all responsible for each other.

Each evening, Said helps his older brother milk the camels. A young calf is usually brought to its mother to start the milking. Said then takes the young calf away, so his brother can continue to milk the camel by hand. A large, leather container, is placed under the camel into which the milk flows. When the containers of milk are filled, he gives them to the women, who process some of the liquid into butter and cheese. Much of the milk is used by the caravan family. Surplus butter and cheese are sold or traded to passing caravans or oasis villagers. Often Said accompanies his brother on the short side trips to nearby oases to trade the butter and cheese before the products spoil. Said

LA MAURITANIE EN MARCHE

The tea ceremony symbolizes hospitality and welcome. Men of the caravan share news and gossip about their recent travels as they renew old friendships.

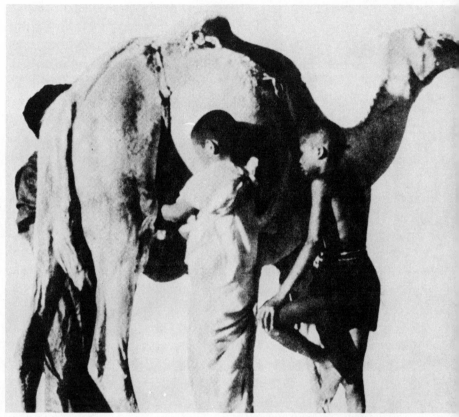

Said helps his older brother milk the camels.

LA REPUBLIQUE ISLAMIQUE DE MAURITANIA

has always enjoyed the traveling life of the desert.

At different times of the year, Said's family meets other nomadic caravan people from the same clan. When these caravans meet, they usually camp near each other for several days. It is a time for the women and men of each caravan to exchange news of the passing year and renew old friendships.

Said recalled the friendly caravan they had spotted the night before. Quickly, arrangements had been made by the men of Said's caravan to hold a tea ceremony for the fellow clansmen of the other caravan. It was to take place in the tent of Said's father. Since Said is considered an adult, he took part in the tea ceremony.

Hot coals were prepared for the fire, and soon the friends appeared at the entrance to the large tent. Greetings were extended by both groups for a long period of time. Then everyone was seated about the floor of the tent while Said's father began making the first cups of tea, which symbolize hospitality and welcome. Mint leaves, green tea, and several heavy lumps of sugar were placed in the boiling water. Each guest was then served a small cup of the hot, spicy, sweet tea. The men shared their news and gossip of recent travels. Then a second round of tea was served —this tea even sweeter and more syrupy than before. The men relaxed more, some reclining on the soft carpets and skins that adorned the floor of the host's tent. The third round of tea was made even sweeter than the second. Following the third round, Said's mother signaled the men. A fine variety of foods awaited them for their main evening meal. The men lingered on long into the night, sharing adventure stories and tales of old.

The leader of the friendly caravan, Mohammed, had told Said's father about a salt deposit that his men had discovered not far from their present campsite. Mohammed had decided to share this discovery with his friends. The next day, strong, young men from both caravans would set out into the desert to dig for salt slabs.

The following morning, Said arose early. He had completed his chores before most of the older men were even awake. As the sun was rising into the sky, Said and a group of twenty men and boys left the campsite. After traveling about two hours, they reached the site of the salt deposits. Said looked around but could not tell what had attracted the sharp-eyed Mohammed to this spot. When Said asked, Mohammed only laughed politely, saying, "When you have lived in the desert as long as your father and I have, you too will know what signs of the desert give such secrets away!"

Long, sharp wooden sticks were taken from several of the supply camels. Men began to push the sand back from the surface with these shovel-like sticks. Several feet below the surface of the sand, the men began to hit the hard, brittle layer of salt deposits. The younger boys used their hands to help clear the sand from the wide area the men wanted exposed. Once that task was accomplished, the sharp, pointed sticks were pounded against the brittle crust of the salt. Slabs about two feet wide and three feet long were broken from the main crust. As these slabs were loosened from the earth, the younger men carried them to the camels. Then the older men carefully secured the slabs to the backs of the camels.

These salt slabs would supply the caravans with salt for at least six months. Such a find was most rewarding to these nomadic travelers because salt was a hard-to-find necessity in the dry desert.

Salt deposits often occur in desert areas where heat causes moisture to evaporate in the rainy season faster than it can be absorbed by the ground. Crystallized salt is then left in the ground. Over the centuries, salt deposits build up into thick layers. Once enough salt had been taken, the men carefully recovered the site with sand. In another six months, they would return for a fresh supply.

To show his family's appreciation to Mohammed for sharing the salt discovery, Said's father had a young goat killed and cooked that night. Great celebrations lasted through the night. It was a happy time. Said's father was enjoying himself thoroughly, and so was Said. These visi-

LA MAURITANIE EN MARCHE

Aziza, and many other Mauritanian girls, attend the public school in town.

tors had been friends for many years, Said thought. It was nice to meet them in the desert and share fine food and companionship. Where else would this take place? Said thinks to himself. He believes, like his father and ancestors before him, that he belongs in the desert. It is his land —the land of the Moors.

AZIZA OF NOUADHIBOU

Aziza's parents have lived in the area of Nouadhibou for almost ten years. In fact, they met and married in Nouadhibou during the first year Aziza's mother worked for the Miferma Mining Com-

pany. Aziza's mother originally lived in Rosso, near the Senegal River. As a young girl, she had opportunities to travel to many parts of Africa and Europe. She was educated in Senegalese schools, and she received commercial training during her secondary school days in France. Aziza's father is a Frenchman who came to work in the engineering division of the Miferma Mining Company.

Although Aziza was brought up as a Protestant, she knows a great deal about the Muslim religion. Many of her friends and acquaintances are Muslims. Aziza attends a public school in the town, where she is in the sixth grade. Classes are con-

31

ALLAN CARPENTER

When Aziza travels to the seashore with her mother, she likes to collect seashells from the ocean waters along the beaches after high tide.

ducted in both French and Arabic. The school day is long, starting at 8 A.M. and lasting until almost 5 P.M. Aziza is a good student, and her mother encourages her to take an active part in all school work.

Many of the older Muslim families in Mauritania are not sure that women should take active public roles in the affairs of the country. Aziza has heard her friends' mothers talk about this, so she asked her own mother what she thought.

Aziza's mother was quick to point out that Mauritania is a new nation, and it needs the help of all its citizens—both men and women. Many younger women are joining forces to help liberate the women of Mauritania from the sheltered, restrictive lives they lead. That is one reason why Aziza's mother is so active in the women's political organizations of Nouadhibou.

Aziza often accompanies her mother on trips to women's groups in nearby villages.

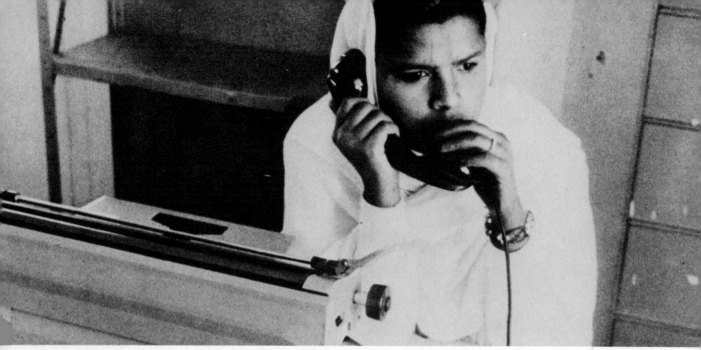

LA MAURITANIE EN MARCHE

Young Mauritanian women, like this one, are beginning to work outside the home.

While her mother attends the meetings, Aziza plays with the village girls. Aziza enjoys the bus rides through the countryside. The buses are always packed with both people and animals. Aziza especially enjoys the meetings in villages near the seashore, when she collects seashells from the ocean waters along the beaches. She and her girl friends trade seashells from their collections. Aziza has a book that she uses to identify the various shells. There are so many varieties to be found along the beach! Aziza knows that the best time for shell hunting is just after the high tide has receded. At this time, hundreds of new shells lay on the beach. Aziza is always thrilled by her visits to the ocean.

At home in Nouadhibou, Aziza spends much time in the school library, trying to learn as much as she can about Paris. Her parents plan to spend their next vacation visiting her father's relatives in France. Many of Aziza's classmates were born in France; some are only staying in Mauritania for a short time. Their parents work with the mining company and are often transferred to other parts of the world. Aziza meets and loses many new friends in this school because of the mining company's employment practices. Aziza has heard her friends tell of the vast differences between France and Mauritania. On her vacation, she will learn all about France for herself. Aziza is certain that she will like France, and she hopes that someday she can go to a university there. She would like to become a doctor and return to help the people of Mauritania.

Mauritania Yesterday

Thousands of years ago Mauritania probably had a semitropical climate and the people living there were mainly farmers. The Negroid people who live in southern Mauritania today might be descendants of these farmers. It is thought that the early inhabitants were forced south in order to maintain their agricultural way of life.

The climatic changes that must have occurred in this area took place over thousands of years, beginning about 2500 B.C. As the land became more desertlike, it was almost impossible for people of ancient times to travel into the depths of the Sahara, as they had once done along well-defined cart tracks. By the time of Christ, people lived on the fringe areas of the desert. Berber tribesmen occupied many villages throughout the Atlas Mountains of North Africa. People also lived in the oases not far inland in what is today Mauritania.

THE CAMEL REVOLUTION

In the third century A.D., Arabs from the Middle East introduced the camel to the people of North Africa. The camel freed the early Berbers of their dependency on the land. No longer were they restricted in their ability to move about. The camel

By the fourth and fifth centuries, many groups wandered the desert land using camels for their transportation. Because a camel can last up to eight days without water, the desert people could move about at will.

enabled them to travel vast distances because it can last for up to eight days without water—or longer if moist desert plants are available.

Because of this new-found freedom, many Berbers who were unhappy with the ruling classes of North Africa retreated into the desert for their own safety and protection. To some the desert was an ideal place. It opened up a vast new territory for those Berbers who felt oppressed in the more restricted border lands.

The Sanhadja Berber people, who moved to the desert of Mauritania, soon began using the camel for themselves. By the fourth and fifth centuries, many groups of them wandered about the desert lands, tending their flocks and establishing a nomadic way of life. They developed extensive trading routes that crisscrossed the Sahara from the Ghana empire of southeastern Mauritania to the cities of Cairo (Egypt) and Fez (Morocco) in the north. Other routes were developed east and west, connecting the Red Sea to the Atlantic Ocean. To many the desert was a forbidding place, but to others it became a retreat, a haven, and a home.

The Ghana empire on the desert fringes to the south was one of the earliest and most famous states in Africa. It endured for about eight hundred years—from the fourth century A.D. to the mid-thirteenth century. Ruled by Sarakole people (some of whose descendants live in southern Mauritania today), Ghana profited by its strategic location between the salt mines of the desert and gold in the West African highlands. The Ghana empire dominated the trade of the western Sudanic area. Its capital at Kumbi Saleh (in modern Mali) was widely known for its wealth and size.

THE SPREAD OF ISLAM

During the eighth and ninth centuries, the Islamic faith spread rapidly across North Africa. Arab conquerors from the Middle East had steadily moved westward, taking over many new lands and imposing the Islamic religion on the local people. Not everyone, however, accepted the Islamic faith. Those who refused were classified as "nonbelievers," and a special tax was placed upon them. According to North African Islamic belief, nonbelievers could be put into slavery. The tribesmen of the Sanhadja, Tuareg, and Teda groups in what is now Mauritania were slow to accept Islam. Like their Berber relations, they grouped together in a confederacy against Arab intrusion. Little by little, however, Islam made its impact, and gradually, most North Africans accepted this religion.

Muslim believers are expected to make a holy pilgrimage to the city of Mecca, where Islam began. When one Sanhadja leader returned from his holy pilgrimage to Mecca, he was accompanied by a noted Islamic scholar, Ibn Yasin. He taught the

These young Moorish boys attend primary school near Nouadhibou.

36

BAREFOOT THROUGH MAURITANIA

Nomad families have survived in the desert for centuries.

people a strict, new version of Islam that was not accepted by orthodox Muslims.

At first, many tribesmen resisted the preachings of Ibn Yasin, but soon he began to gather a strong number of faithful followers, called *murabituns* ("people of the ribat") because they made their headquarters in an isolated, fortified type of monastery called a *ribat*. The Murabituns became a powerful group. They vowed to consecrate their lives to the glory of Allah and to spread His word, even if war were necessary to achieve conversions. The followers of Ibn Yasin grew strong and powerful; his forces traveled north and

east. Not only were mass conversions to Islam achieved, but much fighting and turmoil also resulted, as orthodox Muslim rulers resisted Ibn Yasin's puritanical doctrines.

The northern forces came to be called the *Almoravids,* a variation of the name al-Murabitun. They developed an empire that included not only Morocco and Algeria, but Spain as well. Their civilization flourished for centuries. They established universities and passed on knowledge of medicine and mathematics to medieval Europe. The eastern forces eventually overthrew the Ghana empire and brought about mass converts to Islam in West Africa.

Ibn Yasin never lived to see the full extent of his influence on the people of Mauritania. In 1059 he was killed in battle. Soon after his death, many miracles were reported, which people claimed were the direct influence of Ibn Yasin. He was believed to be an Islamic saint. Even today, many Muslims venerate his tomb. Eventually, Islam became as much a part of the desert people's culture as their nomadic travels were. By the middle of the fifteenth century, Islam was firmly established throughout Mauritania.

The Negroid people of the Senegal River valley had developed a very different way of life than the desert peoples. They chose to remain on the land, cultivating its rich soil. Although most of these people were also converted to Islam, they were often the victims of raids and attacks from nomadic desert bands seeking both slaves and food crops. The river people established their own kingdoms such as Tekrur, which was well established by the thirteenth and fourteenth centuries. The river did not separate the people; instead, it bound them together. The Fulbe, Tokolor, and Sarakole lived peacefully together for many years along this river valley.

By the seventeenth century, additional bands of Arabs from North Africa had invaded the desert lands of Mauritania. For thirty years, the people of the Sanhadja confederacy fought against these Arab intruders. Eventually, they settled down to a more peaceful existence. Tribes often intermingled, and intermarriage was common. Many desert people were a mixture of Arab, Berber, and Negroid; these people were called *Moors.*

MAURITANIA'S MANY NAMES

The land that is now Mauritania was called a number of different names throughout history. To the Arab people of North Africa and the Middle East, it was called *Shinqit.* Shinqit is actually an old oasis in West Africa where pilgrims to Mecca would gather before starting off on their holy trip. The Moors of this land called the area *Trab le-bidan,* or "the land of the whites." Centuries later, the French referred to the territory as *Le territoire Mauritanien,* or "the land of the Moors."

THE COMING OF
THE EUROPEANS

Portuguese explorers were probably the first Europeans to visit what is now Mauritania. As early as the fifteenth century, they occupied the island of Arguin as a base of trade with the mainland for gold and slaves. Spanish adventurers later drove off the Portuguese, and in turn were replaced by the Dutch. During trips along the coastal lands of Mauritania, the Dutch recognized the importance of the scrub called *acacia arabica,* which grew profusely on this land. This bush produces gum arabic, useful in the textile-printing process of European cloth making. Because of the gum arabic, the Dutch began a profitable trade. Soon the English and the French were also interested in this area and its trade possibilities.

The French already had strong holdings along West African shores. The settlement of St. Louis in Senegal (founded in 1626) was just south of the area where the Dutch had their gum arabic trading centers. But the French wanted firmer control over mainland trading. In the Treaty of Paris, in 1814, the nations agreed that France would have control over the trade of the western Sahara and the Senegalese coastline. Although France had gained recognition of its rights by other European nations over the coastal fringe, it was many years before France was able to bring the people of Mauritania under its rule.

COLONIZATION

During the early nineteenth century, many French settlers and businessmen moved into the Senegal River valley, which was a natural highway for trade into the interior. The French government had established its administrative headquarters for the territory in St. Louis, Senegal. Few attempts were made at first by the French to penetrate the interior of Mauritania.

The river valley people were occasionally raided by nomadic tribesmen from the desert interior, particularly when the river peoples were quarreling among themselves. The desert people were organized into strong groups, whose leaders or chiefs were called *emirs*. Many of these *emirates* (kingdoms) even fought among themselves. Rivalry and raiding were a common part of the nomadic desert life.

The threat of raids annoyed the French traders. In 1850 the emperor of France, Napoleon III, ordered the French colonial leaders to insure France's sovereignty along the Senegal River valley. The emperor asked that the colonial administrators ignore any previous treaties signed

LA MAURITANIE

Warlike guards of tribal chiefs annoyed the French with threats of raids.

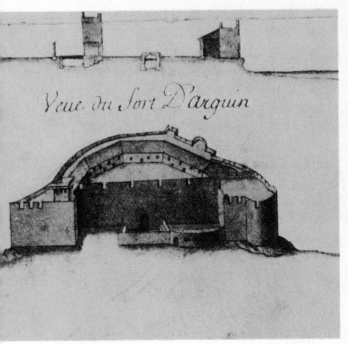

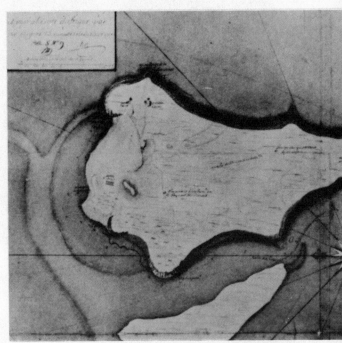

LA MAURITANIE

LA MAURITANIE

Above left: An ancient fort constructed by the Portuguese settlers during the fifteenth century on the island of Arguin. Above right: A map drawn of the island of Arguin in 1722. Below: Women in an emir's camp.

BAREFOOT THROUGH MAURITANIA

with the Africans. France was using its new military superiority to acquire great control over West African trade. At the same time, France felt that territorial conquests would add to the prestige and glory of Napoleon III's regime.

The local colonial governor, Louis Faidherbe, did his best to accomplish these goals. Troops were gathered from local Senegalese villages and trained by the French officers for military duty. Attempts were made to form new treaties with the strongest emirs, to assure continual peace. Some French began to explore the interior of Mauritania. Much in the direction of maintaining peace between the local people and the French was accomplished by Faidherbe. However, he knew that peace would last only as long as the emirs were free to raid the lowlands and then retreat to the safety of their desert highlands.

PENETRATION OF THE INTERIOR

In 1901 the French government established a plan which, if it were successful, would give France total administrative control over Mauritania. A man named Xavier Coppolani was selected to go to Mauritania and make France's plan work.

Coppolani had been raised in Algeria. He knew the Arabic language quite well and was equally knowledgeable of Islamic customs and beliefs. His mission was to gain access to the emirs of the interior plateau region and win their favor, one by one. The French called this strategy "peaceful penetration."

Coppolani went about his task with great vigor. He talked with emirs whose states had been persecuted by stronger emirs. He promised them protection and an annual monetary allowance from the French government if they would agree to be administered by France. To weaker emirs, this plan sounded practical. Coppolani also tried to encourage feuding and rivalry among strong leaders in the same emirship. He even tried to promise some men the title of emir if they would help him overthrow the existing leader. This was an example of the classic colonial policy of "divide and rule."

Coppolani's plans were clever and shrewd, as well as dangerous. Unfortunately for Coppolani, on May 12, 1905, a group of Moorish leaders assassinated him for his interference and troublemaking in their kingdom.

Despite heroic efforts on the part of many Mauritanians, it was not easy to prevent France's takeover. Although Mauritania had no major resources that France could exploit to gain economic wealth, Mauritania had strategic importance as a bridge connecting France's North African and West African colonial possessions. With Mauritania a French possession, no other nation could interfere in any way with French West African development. By the early 1900s, Mauritania had become a part of French West Africa and an official colony of France.

THE FEDERATION OF WEST AFRICA

The federation had little effect on the daily lives of the people of Mauritania. France did very little to improve the region; few, if any, social services were provided. Mauritania's administration was handled from afar, since France used the Senegalese city of St. Louis as headquarters for both colonies.

Many of the emirs of the desert still continued to resist the French when they moved toward the interior. Periodic fighting between the Moors and the French troops took place into the 1930s.

Following World War II, most colonial peoples in Africa began to demand greater participation in the political affairs of their own territory. In 1946 a territorial assembly that included local as well as French people, was established in Mauritania. By 1956, an even stronger form of territorial representation was established. The rising spirit of African nationalism was being recognized all over the continent. The president of France, Charles de Gaulle, tried to accommodate the interests of his French colonies by establishing a French Community in Africa. Colonies in the French Community would become independent states, responsible for managing their own internal affairs. Military and foreign policy, however, would be managed by France. In 1958 Mauritania, along with ten other nations, joined the French Community. Full independence was but a step away.

Mauritanians honor Independence Day with great celebrations.

LA REPUBLIQUE ISLAMIQUE DE MAURITANIA

Mauritania Today

A NEW NATION

With nationhood nearly achieved, the political leaders of Mauritania decided that administrative headquarters must be established within the boundary lines of the country. Selecting the site for the new capital presented many new concerns. The new capital had to be as easily accessible to the Senegal River valley people as to Moorish traders of the north. The site also needed an adequate supply of water in order to maintain the needs of a growing administrative center. Also, it had to be close to communication and transportation links. And no one wanted to establish a new city in the harsh climate of the interior desert. Finally, it was decided that the capital would be built on the hillside near the old town of Nouakchott. The city would be near the ocean—midway between the farms of the south and mines of the north. It would straddle the highway that connects Mauritania with Senegal and Algeria—the Trans-Mauritanian Highway.

No sooner were the first building blocks laid for the site of the new capital than negotiations were opened with France for the final steps toward independence. On November 28, 1960, the Islamic Republic of Mauritania was declared an independent nation.

LED BY A YOUNG LAWYER

Moktar Ould Daddah was overwhelmingly supported and elected by his

The National Assembly building in Nouakchott.

people as the nation's first president. Raised in a prominent Mauritanian family, Daddah was educated in Islamic studies early in life. Later he continued his schooling in Senegal and in France. As a successful lawyer, Daddah worked hard during the colonial days to insure as much representation and participation of Mauritanians in the affairs of the colony as was possible. It was not surprising that his people supported him in this major new step of nationalism for Mauritania.

PROBLEMS OF NATIONAL UNITY

One of Daddah's first major tasks as president was to insure the cooperation of all of the major interest groups in the land. A number of political parties had been established prior to independence. Daddah felt it was important that these parties cooperate for the benefit of building the nation. Daddah asked that the parties sacrifice their individual goals in favor of a major goal—national unity. He called for all past feuds between desert and lowland emirates to be forgotten. He felt it was time for all of the people to join together to establish a single nation.

The inland Moors had often raided the southern blacks of the south, sometimes conscripting them into slavery. Many people alive when Mauritania first became independent remembered these

The president of Mauritania, Moktar Ould Daddah.

LA MAURITANIE EN MARCHE

A squadron of Mauritanian guards stands at attention.

LA REPUBLIQUE ISLAMIQUE DE MAURITANIA

CULTUREL ARABE   كز الثقافى العربى

Since both languages are used, French and Arabic writing is often seen side by side.

MICHAEL ROBERTS

MICHAEL ROBERTS

Many of the streets in Nouakchott, the capital, are sand or dirt.

raids. Thus, there was great distrust and suspicion. Some of the Moors still treated the blacks of the south as inferior.

The new government had a tremendous task on its hands: to join the two peoples for the first time in their history.

Even the choice of a national language became a major issue. The Moors wanted Arabic, and the southern blacks wanted consideration given to their native languages. French was then established as an official language, and Arabic was chosen as a national language. This solution worked as a compromise between the country's two major divisions.

THE GOVERNMENT

The Islamic Republic of Mauritania acknowledges Islam as the official religion of the land. The constitution, however, guarantees the right of religious freedom to all its citizens.

According to the constitution as revised in 1961, Mauritania has a presidential system of government. The president must be a Muslim. His term of office lasts for a period of five years, at which time he may be reelected. The president selects a number of officials to serve as his Cabinet.

The constitution also provides for a National Assembly. This one-house body enacts legislation. The forty members of the Assembly are elected for five-year terms.

An independent judicial system is also guaranteed by the constitution. The judicial system handles the concerns of both civil and Koranic law, an important part of the Islamic religion.

For ease of administration, Mauritania is divided into twelve regions. A government-appointed officer administers each region.

POLITICAL PARTIES

Mauritania has a one-party system of government. The Mauritanian People's Party, established in 1961, manages the affairs of the government. Controlled by a permanent committee of forty members, this group is led by the secretary-general, President Daddah. He believes that "new developing nations cannot often afford the luxury of multiple parties, as evidenced in Western nations, at a time when national unity is an utmost major priority." So the Mauritanian People's Party attempts to accommodate all of the wishes of the different interest groups within the organization.

INDEPENDENCE DAY —NOVEMBER 28

Since the Islamic Republic of Mauritania is a new nation, it honors its Independence Day with great celebrations. Usually the nation's green-and-yellow flag is displayed in all major buildings and many homes and shops. Parades and athletic competitions are held as part of a political rally. The president usually makes a major address to the people, acknowledging the fine work achieved in the past year and

MAURITANIA

BAIE DU
LÉVRIER

INCHIRI

TIRIS-ZEMMOUR

A D R A R

T A G A N T

T R A R Z A

B R A K N A

ASSÂBA

GORGOL

GUIDIMAKA

HODH
OCCIDENTAL

H O D H

O R I E N T A L

Administrative Divisions

asking for their continued support and help in the new year ahead.

INTERNATIONAL COOPERATION

Immediately following its independence, the Islamic Republic of Mauritania applied to the United Nations for membership. At that time, Morocco objected to Mauritania's claim to independence. According to Moroccan interpretation of old treaties, much of the land of Mauritania supposedly belonged to Morocco. The discovery of rich iron reserves in Mauritania also spurred Moroccan claims. This opposition, however, did not prevent Mauritania from becoming an active member of the United Nations in 1969. But it did provide several years of bitter disagreement between the two northwest African nations. In more recent times, however, this neighborly disagreement has been peacefully settled.

Mauritania is also an active member of the Organization of African Unity (OAU). In 1970 President Daddah was selected as chairman of the OAU. This was a great honor and sign of respect for this African leader, who has done much to bring his nation's people together.

EDUCATION

Traditionally, the leaders of the mosque helped young people to speak Arabic and learn enough about the Koran to be loyal Islamic followers. For most, the rest of their education involved learning the family trade; most youths worked side by side with their elders as they were growing up. So formal education, as known in the Western world, is rather new to Maurita-

These children attend school in a large urban area.

LA MAURITANIE EN MARCHE

nia. Many Mauritanians feel it is of little value now, but others argue that it is necessary for the future.

Public education is available at the elementary and secondary school levels. Instruction is in both Arabic and French. The schools' curriculum is like that in French schools, with the addition of Islamic studies. To assist the vast number of nomadic families, the government sometimes sends a teacher along with a large caravan of nomadic herders. The teacher sets up his tent and conducts classes part of each day. When it is time for the nomads to travel on, the teacher goes along, too. This system is a start in providing nomad youngsters with a formal education.

The secondary school curriculum has two tracks. One is a brief course for students who do not plan to go to college, and the other is a longer program for university-bound students. Presently, there are no universities in Mauritania; students must leave the country in order to complete their education.

There is an acute shortage of skilled workers in Mauritania. Usually companies must bring in personnel from neighboring African nations, while many of Mauritania's unskilled citizens remain unemployed. Several vocational programs in mining, veterinary, and agricultural skills have recently been developed because the need is great for semiskilled and skilled workers in Mauritania.

The government is very concerned about the literacy rate of its people. Only 10 percent of the nation's youth attend school. The government spends a substantial portion of its annual budget to improve opportunities for education for all of Mauritania's citizens.

BAREFOOT THROUGH MAURITANIA

Children of nomadic families often have a teacher traveling with them to conduct classes.

Natural Treasures

THE SEARCH

Water and grass for grazing are the two items continuously sought after by the nomadic herders of Mauritania's desert lands. In a region where such items are scarce, one of the greatest treasures to a nomadic herdsman is the oasis, where humans and animals alike can find both grass and water.

Usually an oasis gets its water from sources far below the surface of the earth. Date palms flourish in these watered lands, providing both shade and fruit for the inhabitants of the oasis. Often smaller vegetable crops are grown about the base of the date palms. The date palm has long been considered an important fruit of the desert. Its fruit is light in weight, is easily stored, and is quite nourishing.

Scattered about the desert are dwarf grasses and shrubs, used by herders to help feed their animals. Cushion plants, tamarisk, succulents, and thorny acacia trees are also found in certain areas of the desert.

ANIMALS

The desert provides a home to many interesting birds and animals. One of the largest birds in the world, the ostrich, is often found where vegetation is sparse. The bird sometimes grows as tall as nine feet. Its fluffy black, white, and pinkish plumes have often been used by local Africans for decorative items. In ancient

An oasis is a great treasure to a nomadic herdsman. Water and grass can be found here for both humans and animals.

times, the Arabs of North Africa used the fat of the ostrich as an ointment for certain diseases. The ostrich cannot fly and has adapted itself as a ground bird. A very fast bird, the ostrich can run about thirty miles an hour, which is faster than a horse! Ostriches run with their wings outstretched. They protect themselves from other animals by kicking with their strong feet. A blow to the chest of a man by an ostrich is reportedly strong enough to kill the man.

Another interesting bird of the dry desert is the bustard. More than twenty-two species of bustards are known to man, varying in size from that of a chicken to that of a large turkey. The greater bustard and the lesser bustard are the species commonly found in Africa. The greater bustard weighs up to thirty-two pounds. The bustard, with black-streaked yellow feathers on the back and grayish-white feathers in front, is often seen walking about with other grazing animals. Since the bustard enjoys eating insects, it slyly lets the moving hooves of grazing animals frighten insects into the air. Then the bustard snatches the insects in midair. Bustards also eat small reptiles.

The deadly poisonous sand viper also makes its home in the desert. Legend says that a similar snake caused the death of the famous Queen Cleopatra of ancient Egypt. Another poisonous animal, the scorpion, is also at home in this land, and appears in many varieties.

An interesting animal of the savanna lands near the desert is the fennec. A small, foxlike creature, its body is barely eight inches long, though its creamy-white, bushy tail brings the total length of the animal to just over one foot—about half the size of an ordinary house cat. With large, pointed ears, the fennec usually makes its home in a burrow scooped out of the light, sandy soil.

The fennec is reputed to be elusive and clever. An Arabic saying goes: "Two dogs make a fennec play, three make him laugh, four make him run about, five make him flee, and six dogs finally catch him." The fennec is noctural, sleeping during the day and going out at night to hunt its food. It enjoys eating the date fruit and is able to climb the tall palm trees to fetch its supply of fruit.

In the more tropical green belt of the Senegal River, cheetah, panthers, lions, elephants, and hippopotamuses are sometimes found. Crocodiles can be seen along some parts of the river. With increasing human population in this vicinity, however, the concentration of wildlife has gradually diminished. These larger animals need a vast area in which to graze and migrate. As the country's human population grows, it might not be able to retain its wildlife population at a stable level.

Off the shores of northern Mauritania, both warm- and cold-water currents meet in the ocean—making ideal spawning grounds for fish. The fishing grounds off the Mauritanian coast are considered by some as the best in the world. Great Atlantic sharks are occasionally sighted in

LA REPUBLIQUE ISLAMIQUE DE MAURITANIA

Tending herds of sheep, goats, oxen, donkeys, and camels is part of the nomadic way of life.

LA REPUBLIQUE ISLAMIQUE DE MAURITANIA

LA REPUBLIQUE ISLAMIQUE DE MAURITANIA

55

LA MAURITANIE EN MARCHE

Some of the best fishing in the world is found off the Mauritanian coast.

these waters. The giant whale shark often comes to feed on the flourishing supply of plankton. Fishing fleets from many parts of the world come to harvest the valuable array of fish treasures in these waters.

MINERALS

At present, very little is known about the minerals underneath Mauritania. Despite some early explorations for oil, no significant discoveries have yet been made. It is known that there are extensive deposits of iron ore and copper. Gypsum and titanium deposits have also been located. Exploration continues, and perhaps other valuable treasures of the land will be discovered.

An oil refinery on the coast.

MICHAEL ROBERTS

The People Live in Mauritania

A NOMADIC POPULATION

Mauritania's population is estimated at about one million people. Population figures vary because no official census has been taken in the new nation. An estimated 70 percent of the people lead nomadic lives. With so many people constantly on the move, accurate population figures are difficult to determine.

Of the total population, about 80 percent of the people are Moors. The remaining 20 percent are mostly blacks, a mixture of Fulbe, Sarakole, Wolof, Bambara, and Tokolor. About two thousand French also reside in Mauritania.

The distribution of people in the nation varies greatly according to region. Only 10 percent of the total population lives in the cities or towns. Another 16 percent farm in the Senegal River valley. Nomads roam along the south and southeastern stretches of the Senegal River valley, but not as near to the river as the settled farmers. Gradually, many desert nomads have been migrating farther south, especially during times of drought. Thus, the severe increases in numbers of people and herds on the southern lands have overextended the land's use and caused erosion problems. In some areas this problem is only temporary, but elsewhere it has become permanent. It seems as if the desert is slowly inching southward, and many nations that border on the desert have become very concerned about this problem.

During the first ten years following independence, several towns and cities were built and developed. These boys are watching a concrete mixer used for new construction.

INTERNATIONAL BANK FOR RECONSTRUCTION AND DEVELOPMENT

UNITED NATIONS

Above: The interior of a Moorish dwelling. Below left: Mauritanians are hardy people who have learned how to survive in the desert. Below right: This woman has used a red tint to decorate her hands.

LA REPUBLIQUE ISLAMIQUE DE MAURITANIA

LA REPUBLIQUE ISLAMIQUE DE MAURITANIA

LA REPUBLIQUE ISLAMIQUE DE MAURITANIA   LA REPUBLIQUE ISLAMIQUE DE MAURITANIA

Above left: A small number of people, like this girl, live and farm near the Senegal River. Above right: The majority of the people, like this girl, are nomads.

The vast number of nomads are not as conscious of the "new nationalism" of Africa, and they find the border regulations difficult to contend with. To them, the desert is the land of the Moors, and it has no boundaries.

THE MOORS

Within Moorish society, there has developed a strong caste system. The major distinctions between Moors is that of a "white Moor" and a "black Moor." Supposedly, this difference has nothing to do with skin color but with one's status in Moorish society. Black Moors are descendants of those people who were once slaves of other Moors (white Moors) or freed slaves employed by the white Moors. Even in Moorish society today white Moors feel strongly superior to black Moors. Although slavery has been absolutely forbidden by the constitution of 1961, some people believe that the caste system of Moorish life still functions as a type of slavery in the nomadic life of the Moors.

The Moors have been at home in the

LA MAURITANIE EN MARCHE

Although the Moors work hard, they do have time to relax in the desert.

62

MICHAEL ROBERTS

The mosque is the Muslim's place of worship.

desert for hundreds of years. They have avoided the more humid regions of the south, as well as the coastal stretches along Mauritania's western border. Nomadic Moors usually carry all their possessions with them. The large tents that provide the people's evening shelter are made from a framework of wooden poles usually covered with camel or goat skins. The framework is structured so it can be easily dismantled and packed on camels for the trip to the next campsite.

The eldest man in each "tent" or extended family group is usually the leader. He is expected to make decisions about the tent's seasonal movements. He is responsible for distributing the tent's income to the individuals and for assigning and supervising work duties for each person. According to Muslim tradition, his wealth and leadership are usually passed on to his eldest son.

THE RELIGION OF ISLAM

Islam plays an important part in the life of Mauritanians. The nomadic Moors are just as tied to this faith as the more permanently settled inhabitants. The nomad does not need a mosque to offer his prayers to Allah. Five times a day, he offers prayers according to the Islamic tradition; at dawn, noon, late afternoon, sunset, and night. The *faithful,* or followers of Islam, usually carry small prayer mats, which they lay out on the desert sands. Then, facing toward Mecca, they recite prayers from the Koran.

The Islamic religion is based on five main points, called the "Five Pillars." A

LA REPUBLIQUE ISLAMIQUE DE MAURITANIA

Although most of Mauritania's fish is consumed locally, about one-third is exported.

Muslim is asked to declare his acceptance of Allah, of Mohammed as his Prophet, and of the Koran as Allah's word. Second, a Muslim is asked to pray daily. The prayers are usually said facing east—toward Mecca, the birthplace of Mohammed. Thus, Mecca is considered by Muslims as the holiest of cities. Third, a Muslim is asked to give alms. This act is supposed to help purify one's remaining wealth. Fourth, a Muslim is asked to fast during certain holy seasons of the year. Last, a person is asked to make a holy pilgrimage to Mecca once in his lifetime. A person who has made the holy pilgrimage is a *haji*. The title "al-Hājj" would be used in front of his name.

For the nomad, Islam has been his primary form of education, dictating his life's laws and actions. The Koran explains to Muslims how they should live. When problems arise, a holy man trained in the law of the Koran usually settles the dispute. Muslim faithful all over the world accept the Koran as the final law.

THE BLACK MINORITIES OF THE SOUTH

Although few in number compared to the Moors, the people of southern Mauritania are no less important. The Fulbe are pastoral people who roam the savanna grasslands that parallel the Senegal River. They are great cattle herders who usually establish temporary villages in a good grazing area. Small beehive-type huts are constructed, some for the people to sleep in and others to store the cattle's grain and supplies. When the group is ready to move

LA MAURITANIE EN MARCHE

To celebrate Independence Day, this young man wears a shirt with Mauritania's symbols.

LA MAURITANIE EN MARCHE

Because of the warm climate, Mauritanians can spend much time out of doors.

Some Moors have moved to urban areas because they feel there are more opportunities for their children.

on to fresh grasslands, the huts are abandoned. Sometimes they are used on return trips.

The Sarakole people live along the Senegal River valley. They claim to have been the first people to live in Mauritania on this river. It is thought that long-ago ancestors of the Sarakole may have been the original creators of the Ghana empire. Many folktales relate the Sarakole to these early days of glory.

Other groups of people from related West African tribes have also settled in this river valley. The valley's good soil and growing conditions have made it an excellent place to live and farm. Although new national borders have divided the Senegal River between Mauritania and Senegal, the river people live as if no border existed. They fish, farm, and trade as if the river valley, both sides included, was their nation.

PROBLEMS OF URBANIZATION

Several towns and cities rapidly developed in the first ten years following independence. The new capital, Nouakchott, has provided jobs for many semiskilled and skilled workers. Since its expansion, old Port Etienne (now called Nouadhibou) also provides many skilled-labor jobs. The mining areas of the north provide still more jobs for skilled workers. Lower-caste people of Moorish society see the new urban centers as opportunities to provide a better way of life for themselves. But training and education is often needed to turn these willing workers into skilled tradesmen—and training takes

LA MAURITANIE EN MARCHE

In Mauritania, many workers are learning new skills.

time. Adjusting to staying in one place all the time is also difficult for many of these nomads. In the meantime, skilled workers from neighboring nations are often brought into Mauritania to fill many jobs in the new industries.

THE MOORS AND THE RIVER PEOPLE

Problems have developed between the Moors of the north and the black people of the south. The river people want as much governmental recognition as their northern neighbors have. Antagonistic feelings of past feuds and slave raids are still in the minds of some people. The feelings and attitudes of "master" and "slave" are voiced in some complaints against the government. The black people resented the institution of Arabic as a national language, arguing that their native languages should be considered as well. To insure opportunities for their children in education, government, and industry, French was offered as an official language for the nation, in addition to Arabic as a national language. Southerners also want more representation in the National Assembly. These conflicts are gradually being solved.

The People Work in Mauritania

SUBSISTENCE ECONOMY

Animal husbandry, the largest occupation in Mauritania, is part of the nomadic way of life. Sheep, goats, cattle, and camels have historically been tended by the majority of Mauritania's inhabitants. The next important occupation in Mauritania is agriculture. These two occupations, however, are conducted at what is called a *subsistence level* of economy: the people raise only enough cattle or grow only enough crops to satisfy their basic needs for living. Little, if any, surplus is acquired. Enough trading occurs between the herders and the farmers so each can acquire the staples, or necessities, of life. Life has been almost unchanged for most of Mauritania's people for hundreds of years.

Farmers produce millet, dates, beans, corn, yams, watermelons, groundnuts, barley, and rice. Of these crops, dates are the only food produced in quantities large enough for export. Mauritania must import food for its local needs. The government would like to increase the country's food production, decreasing the annual need for imports.

Gum arabic, used for textile printing and other processes, continues to be exported each year. Plans have been made to

These men live a nomadic way of life, moving about with their herd of sheep to find grazing land. Animal husbandry is the largest occupation in Mauritania. Most herders raise only enough cattle for their basic needs and the remainder are sold. Wool sheered from the sheep is used in making carpets.

INTERNATIONAL BANK FOR RECONSTRUCTION AND DEVELOPMENT

Workmen sit, taking a rest, on top of rails used in the construction of the railroads.

LA MAURITANIE EN MARCHE

Railroad cars carry ore across the desert.

expand, plant, and grow many more acacia arabica trees, from which gum arabic is taken, in order to achieve more revenue.

The methods used to grow crops are also receiving the attention of agricultural experts. Experimental procedures are being developed to improve the growing of rice. Control of the flood waters of the Senegal River may also be used to increase the production of other food crops raised in this area. Modern chemical and farming procedures are also being introduced to the local people, and agricultural training sessions educate them about these procedures.

NEW INDUSTRIES

Because Mauritania does no manufacturing, it must import all of its machinery, transportation equipment, construction materials, and petroleum products. But the government wants to develop a more diversified economy for Mauritania. The vast iron deposits found in the north near Fort Gouraud are helping. Since 1952, the Miferma Company has been involved in the mining, transport, and export of this valuable ore.

The Miferma Company needed to transport the rich ore to the seacoast, where it could be shipped to foreign buyers. The country's road system was not adequate for the mine's steady demands. So the company built a railroad more than four hundred miles long to meet this need. This heavy-duty railway is the second-strongest in the world.

Carting the iron ore from Fort Gouraud to the ocean port of Nouadhibou takes about eighteen hours. There the unloading and loading operations are almost completely automated. This might seem to be a rather modern technical advancement for what might be considered a very underdeveloped nation, but Miferma felt it was a necessary one. Mauritania lacked the semiskilled and skilled labor force to meet the company's needs.

Even with this automation, the mining and shipping operations have created jobs for more than four thousand people. Two new villages have been built to accommodate Miferma employees. The iron ore accounts for 75 percent of Mauritania's exports. The government receives a 52.5 percent share of the ore revenues.

Another important source of income is expected from the copper mines at Akjoujt. At first, the facility lacked enough water to make the mining operation successful. Other methods of processing the copper ore were developed and mining is now feasible. The road network was improved. Truckers now move the processed ore overland to the new port facilities at Nouakchott. Many new jobs will also be provided by this industry.

The copper mines at Akjoujt. Next to iron, copper is the most useful of all metals. It is soft, tough, resistant to corrosion, and easily shaped by machines. Copper is an excellent conductor of electricity and heat.

LA REPUBLIQUE ISLAMIQUE DE MAURITANIA

LA MAURITANIE EN MARCHE

Both warm- and cold-water currents meet in the ocean, making ideal spawning grounds for fish.

76

UNITED NATIONS

Sun-dried fish are exported to West African ports.

77

Fishing is another important source of wealth to Mauritania. Recognizing the vast potential of the fishing waters off the coast of Nouadhibou, a new fish-processing and freezing plant has been opened in that area. Although most of Mauritania's fish is consumed locally, about one-third is exported.

TRANSPORTATION

Transportation is one of Mauritania's greatest handicaps to current industrial development. Of the eighteen hundred miles of roads that exist in the country, only about two hundred miles are paved. The rest are rough dirt tracks, which prove extremely dangerous and unreliable, as windstorms and floods often erase the tracks. Thus, the wear and tear on vehicles is extreme. Heavy-duty vehicles are used primarily, but even those must come with adequate repair parts, oversized gas tanks, and other precautionary equipment. A jeep is said to last only ten months under such hard conditions!

The Trans-Mauritanian Highway is the nation's main road. Mostly unpaved, it connects Senegal in the south to Algeria in the north. Ferries are used to cross the Senegal River, but more permanent bridges will probably be built between Senegal and Mauritania as roadwork develops.

Many small landing strips are located throughout the country for airplanes. Air Mauritanie provides small airplane service to many towns in the land. International flights are available through Air Afrique and UTA. The larger air terminal at Nouadhibou has international service.

Seaports have been developed and expanded since independence at both Nouadhibou and Nouakchott to provide for Mauritania's own needs.

At present, the railroad is used only to transport iron ore. Travelers depend on heavy-duty Land Rovers, jeeps, and animals for local transportation. It seems unlikely in the immediate future, though, that the camel will become obsolete, even though better heavy-duty vehicles are being developed.

COMMUNICATIONS

Communication services are provided to the people primarily by radio. Broadcasts in Arabic, French, and other local languages are made daily. Even in remote regions, transistor radios are becoming more commonly seen, bringing the news of the world into nomadic camps. But the visiting nomad probably still provides his friends with as much news as any other source. There is no television in Mauritania. Bilingual bulletins are published by the

The vast iron deposits found in the north near Fort Gouraud are helping to strengthen the economy. The Miferma Company has been mining, transporting, and exporting this ore. To get the ore to the seacoast, a railroad more than four hundred miles long was built.

78

MICHAEL ROBERT

Both Nouadhibou and Nouakchott have developed seaports. Above is a pier at Nouakchott. Air Mauritanie (below) services more than twenty-five airports in Mauritania.

LA MAURITANIE EN MARCHE

AIR MAURITANIE ‫يتانية‬

Ministry of Information. Many interesting international newspapers and magazines can be easily purchased in the more developed towns, such as Nouakchott and Nouadhibou.

Three major problems face Mauritania in its economic development. The search for water in this mostly desert nation presents one concern. Roads, railroads, and airstrips must be developed throughout the land. Finally, educational programs must be developed to provide a pool of skilled workers who can be used as new industries are created.

The Enchantment of Mauritania

THE DESERT

Mauritanians are still living a way of life that is deeply rooted in the past. The desert oasis of Atar has been an important oasis trading center since the earliest days of nomadic caravans. The early gold and salt traders brought their heavily laden caravans to this refreshing center. Numerous craftsmen settled near the oasis, perfecting the leather and jewelry crafts. Desert visitors often traded their newly acquired gold or salt for some of these fine products. Much of the same can still be observed in Atar today.

It is not uncommon to see groups of tall, desert Moors approach the oasis on their camels. Many are heavily robed in a variety of colorful garments and decorative ornaments. Some partially cover their faces from the hot rays of the sun and the blowing sands. Some men wear decorative swords or knives on belts around their waist, glittering in the sunlight. Groups of women can be seen at the marketplaces, as well as in the main part of town. Often the women wander in groups, window shopping and enjoying their leisure time.

Mauritanian handicrafts are finely made. For years, craftsmen have produced fine jewelry objects: gold and silver rings, earrings, and pins. Others work with leather, producing brightly dyed leather pieces fashioned into cushions, mats,

Carpet weaving is a new government-sponsored industry in Mauritania. Women do the carding, spinning, and weaving of the wonderful wool from which the famous Mauritanian hand-woven rugs are made.

MICHAEL ROBERTS

Women often are seen talking and shopping in groups at the market, the heart of the community.

MICHAEL ROBERTS

Brightly painted pots are sold in the marketplace.

MICHAEL ROBERTS

Rattan mats are made by local craftsmen.

MICHAEL ROBERTS

MICHAEL ROBERTS

Tailors can be seen at work in the market. One (above) is using a sewing machine. A variety of finished clothing can be bought in the market (below).

MICHAEL ROBERTS

MICHAEL ROBERTS

pouches, and purses. These items are sold in the shops and marketplaces. Young children often help in the shops, learning their parents' trade as an apprentice in the crafts.

SENEGAL VALLEY

The Senegal Valley area is often called "the gateway to sub-Saharan Africa." The land here contrasts greatly with the dry, desert region of the north. The people are physically different from their Moorish neighbors to the north. The Senegal Valley has a black African population, culturally akin to the people of the south and east. Village life around the river is relatively permanent, and development of fishing and farming has tended to unite these valley people.

Although the Senegal River actually separates the two countries of Mauritania and Senegal, the life of the river people is not really divided on national boundary lines. Villagers cross the river to work and shop. In the evening they return from their boats and fields to enjoy a relaxing night. The fresh fires and cooking smells from the many homes add a delightful aroma to the warm night air. Some of the young men of the area participate in canoe races along stretches of the Senegal River, while others sit along the banks and cheer their favorite canoe on to victory. The girls share news of the day with one another as they prepare the evening meal and put the younger children to bed. Often when all the day's chores are done, families gather together and listen to news, current events programs, or relaxing music on the radio.

THE COAST

Mauritania's coastal front is a gorgeous sight to behold. The sandy silver beaches extend for hundreds of miles. It is a haven for sunbathers, swimmers, and fishermen. So far Mauritania has no resort facilities along the coast, but there are limitless possibilities for tourism.

Although much of the land continues as it was for hundreds of years, a new way of life is emerging in the cities. In the capital, Nouakchott, building seems to be going on all the time. People gather here from various corners of the country and congregate about the shops and marketplaces. Schools, mosques, medical dispensaries, and government buildings give the city a feeling of permanence and modernity.

The city of Nouadhibou has a modern ocean port, with automated iron-ore loading facilities at the docks. The fish-processing plant handles all the local fish. The array of smaller fishing vessels, which come and go from this port area, add color and excitement to this rapidly developing coastal area.

Local fishermen brave the rollers in the Atlantic for their catch.

MICHAEL ROBERTS

Young people will play an important part in the future of Mauritania.

FUTURE CHALLENGES

The Islamic Republic of Mauritania faces many challenges to its future growth and development. Its geography, climate, and limited known resources impose severe limits to the possibility of future developments. But the people living in Mauritania have survived in this land for hundreds of years. They are very proud of their traditions and their way of life. Perhaps this pride in themselves is the most important aspect to the future of the country.

Western Sahara was formerly called Spanish Sahara, because it was under Spanish control. In February 1976 Spain gave up control and the name was changed. Western Sahara was annexed to two of its neighbors, Mauritania and Morocco. Mauritania received the southern part of the Rio de Oro Province. There is now a movement in Western Sahara to gain self-determination.

Handy Reference Section

INSTANT FACTS

Political:
Official Name—Islamic Republic of Mauritania
Form of Government—Presidential with unicameral National Assembly
Capital—Nouakchott
Monetary Unit—CFA franc
National Religion—Islam
National Language—Arabic
Official Language—French
Independence Day—November 28
National Flag—Green background with gold star above a gold crescent moon
National Anthem—"Air Traditionnel"
Geographical:
Area—419,000 square miles
Highest Point—2,900 feet above sea level
Lowest Point—sea level

POPULATION

Population—approximately 1,000,000 people
Population Density—1.8 persons per square mile
Population Growth Rate—1-2 percent
Birth Rate (per 1000)—44.4
Death Rate (per 1000)—22.7
Average Life Span—41 years

Population Distribution (approximate):

Moors	800,000
French	2,000
Others	195,000

PRINCIPAL CITIES

Nouakchott	55,000
Nouadhibou	20,000

REGIONS

Adrar
Assaba
Baie du Lévrier
Brakna
Gorgol

Guidimakha
Hodh Occidental
Hodh Oriental
Inchiri
Tagant
Tiris Zemmour
Trarza

YOU HAVE A DATE WITH HISTORY

200-300 A.D.—Camel introduced into Mauritania; Berbers retreat into desert

300-500—Nomadic tribes evolve in Sahara

700-900—Islam spreads to desert

1059—Ibn Yasin killed in battle

1200-1400—Tekrur kingdom flourishes at Senegal River.

1400-1500—Islam firmly established in Mauritania; Portuguese visit area

1647-1677—Thirty Years' War fought between Moors and Arabs

early 1800s—Frenchmen settle Senegal Valley

1814—Treaty of Paris signed; Europeans recognize France's control of Mauritania

1901—Xavier Coppolani begins "peaceful penetration" of interior

1920—Mauritania becomes official French colony, member of French West Africa

1930s—Periodical fighting between French and Moors takes place

1946—Mauritanian territorial assembly begins

1956—Nationalism begins to sweep the country

1958—Mauritania joins French Community

1960—Mauritania becomes completely independent (November 28); Moktar Ould Daddah elected president

1961—Mauritania joins United Nations; constitution revised; Mauritanian People's Party established

1970—President Daddah selected chairman of OAU

Index

About the Authors

With the publication of his first book for school use when he was twenty, **Allan Carpenter** began a career as an author that has spanned more than 135 books—with more still to be published in the Enchantment of Africa series for Childrens Press. After teaching in the public schools of Des Moines, Mr. Carpenter began his career as an educational publisher at the age of twenty-one when he founded the magazine *Teachers Digest*. In the field of educational periodicals, he was responsible for many innovations. During his many years in publishing, he has perfected a highly organized approach to handling large volumes of factual material: after extensive traveling and having collected all possible materials, he systematically reviews and organizes everything. From his apartment high in Chicago's John Hancock Building, Allan recalls: "My collection and assimilation of materials on the states and countries began before the publication of my first book." Allan is the founder of Carpenter Publishing House and of Infordata International, Inc., publishers of *Issues in Education* and *Index to U.S. Government Periodicals*. When he is not writing or traveling, his principal avocation is music. He has been the principal bassist of many symphonies, and he managed the country's leading non-professional symphony for twenty-five years.

Co-author **James W. Hughes** has traveled extensively through over half of the nations of Africa and lived and worked in Kenya for several years. Dr. Hughes has contributed to journals and books in both Africa and the United States. He has served as chairman of the International Activities Committee of the National Council for the Social Studies, and has served as an educational consultant for the International Relations Committee of the National Education Association in both Kenya and Nepal. Dr. Hughes is currently Director of Teacher Education at Oakland University.